The Gigantic Coloring Book of Bible Stories

Illustrated by Rick Incrocci

Standard PUBLISHING

Cincinnati, Ohio

Published by Standard Publishing, Cincinnati, Ohio
www.standardpub.com

Copyright © 2009 by Standard Publishing

95445, Printed in Cincinnati, Ohio for Standard Publishing, August 2009

ISBN 978-0-7847-2359-3

15 14 13 12 11 10 09   2 3 4 5 6

God Created the World

Genesis 1:1–2:3

God made the heavens.

Based on Genesis 1:7, 8

**God named the dry land Earth,
and the water Seas.**

Based on Genesis 1:10

**God made the larger light to rule the day
and the smaller light to rule the night.**

Based on Genesis 1:16

**God made all the creatures
that move in the oceans.**

Based on Genesis 1:21

God made every kind of bird that flies.

Based on Genesis 1:21

God blessed all the creatures he had made.

Based on Genesis 1:22

On the seventh day God rested.

Based on Genesis 2:2, 3

God Created Man and Woman

Based on Genesis 2:7–3:24

God made a man from the dust of the ground.

Based on Genesis 2:7

**God made a garden called Eden,
and put the man there.**

Based on Genesis 2:8

God told the man he could eat from any tree in the garden except the tree of the knowledge of good and evil.

Based on Genesis 2:16, 17

Adam gave names to all the animals and birds.

Based on Genesis 2:20

God made a woman out of one of Adam's ribs so Adam would have a helper.

Based on Genesis 2:20-22

**A serpent tricked the woman into eating
the fruit God said not to eat.**

Based on Genesis 3:1-6

**The woman gave some of the fruit to
her husband, and he ate it too.**

Based on Genesis 3:6

God sent the man and woman out of the garden.

Noah and the Flood

Based on Genesis 6:1–9:17

Noah was a good man who followed God.

Based on Genesis 6:9

God told Noah he was going to destroy the earth because it was full of violence. He told Noah to build a large boat called an ark.

Based on Genesis 6:13, 14

It rained for forty days, and the ark floated above the earth.

Based on Genesis 7:17, 18

Noah sent out a dove to see if the flood waters had gone down.

Based on Genesis 8:8

**That evening the dove returned with
an olive leaf in its beak.**

Noah and his family left the ark.

Based on Genesis 8:18

All the animals left the boat.

Based on Genesis 8:19

**God put a rainbow in the sky as a
promise to never again destroy the earth by water.**

Based on Genesis 9:15-17

The Tower of Babel

**At one time, everyone on earth spoke
the same language.**

Based on Genesis 11:1

**The people decided to build a city and
a tower that would reach Heaven.**

Based on Genesis 11:4

God decided to make the people speak different languages.

Based on Genesis 11:6, 7

God scattered the people all over the earth, and they stopped building the city.

Based on Genesis 11:8, 9

The Story of Abraham

Based on Genesis 12:1–21:8

**God told a man named Abram to leave
his country and his relatives and go to a new land.**

Based on Genesis 12:1

Abram did as God said and left with his wife Sarai and his brother's son Lot.

Based on Genesis 12:4, 5

God promised to give new land to Abram and his family.

Based on Genesis 12:7

God told Abraham that he and Sarah would have a son and that his name would be Isaac.

Based on Genesis 17:19

**When Abraham and Sarah were very old,
they had a son at the exact time God said they would.**

Based on Genesis 21:2

Isaac and Rebekah

Based on Genesis 24:1–25:26

Abraham told his servant to return to the land of their relatives and find a wife for Isaac.

Based on Genesis 24:4

When the servant arrived in Abraham's homeland, he prayed to God.

Based on Genesis 24:10-14

**A beautiful young woman named Rebekah
came to the well and filled her pitcher.**

Based on Genesis 24:15, 16

Abraham's servant ran to Rebekah and asked her for a drink of water from her pitcher.

Based on Genesis 24:17

Rebekah gave the servant a drink of water.
The servant thanked God for keeping his promise.

Based on Genesis 24:18, 26, 27

Rebekah ran to her mother's house and told her family what had happened.

Based on Genesis 24:28

**Rebekah's brother Laban and her father, Bethuel,
told the servant to take Rebekah and
let her marry Isaac as God had said.**

Based on Genesis 24:50, 51

Rebekah became Isaac's wife, and he loved her.

Based on Genesis 24:67

Isaac and Rebekah had twin sons. The first was covered with red hair, so his name was Esau.

Based on Genesis 25:23-25

Isaac and Rebekah named their second son Jacob.

Based on Genesis 25:26

The Story of Jacob

Based on Genesis 28:1–30:24

**Isaac sent Jacob to live
with Rebekah's brother Laban.**

Based on Genesis 28:1-5

**That evening Jacob stopped.
He lay down and went to sleep.**

Based on Genesis 28:11

Jacob dreamed about a ladder that reached all the way to Heaven.

Based on Genesis 28:12

In Jacob's dream, God said he would protect Jacob and bring him back to the land where Isaac lived.

Based on Genesis 28:15

Jacob went on his journey to the land of the people of the East.

Based on Genesis 29:1

Jacob came upon three flocks of sheep getting water from the well.

Based on Genesis 29:2, 3

While Jacob was speaking with the shepherds, Rachel came with her father's sheep.

Based on Genesis 29:9

Rachel's father let her marry Jacob.

Based on Genesis 29:28

Jacob had many children.

Based on Genesis 29:32-35; 30:1-24

The Story of Joseph

Based on Genesis 37:1–41:57

Jacob loved Joseph, his youngest son.
He gave Joseph a coat of many colors.
Joseph's brothers were jealous.

Based on Genesis 37:3, 4

**Joseph's brothers were caring for the sheep. Jacob
sent Joseph to see if everything was okay.**

Based on Genesis 37:14

Joseph found his brothers in Dothan.

Based on Genesis 37:17

Joseph's brothers threw him in a pit. One of the brothers, Judah, talked the others into selling him to some traders.

Based on Genesis 37:24-27

The traders took Joseph to Egypt to be a slave.

Based on Genesis 37:28, 36

Joseph's brothers took Joseph's coat and put blood on it. Then they took it to their father.

Based on Genesis 37:31, 32

**In Egypt, God was with Joseph and made
him successful in all that he did.**

Based on Genesis 39:3

The king of Egypt realized Joseph was very wise, so he put him in charge of the entire land.

Based on Genesis 41:39-41

The Birth of Moses

Based on Exodus 1:1–2:10

**There was a new king who came to power in Egypt.
He knew nothing of all the good Joseph had done.**

Based on Exodus 1:8

The new king ordered that all the baby boys of Hebrew mothers be killed.

Based on Exodus 1:16

A Hebrew woman had a baby boy, but after three months she could no longer hide him.

Based on Exodus 2:2, 3

The baby boy's mother made a basket out of reeds and covered it with tar so it would float.

**The baby boy's mother put him in the
basket and placed it by the bank.**

Based on Exodus 2:3

The baby's sister watched to see what would happen.

Based on Exodus 2:4

**The king's daughter came down
to wash herself in the river.**

Based on Exodus 2:5

**The princess saw the basket and
sent her maid to get it.**

Based on Exodus 2:5

**When the princess opened the basket, she
saw the baby. The baby was crying and
the princess felt sorry for him.**

Based on Exodus 2:6

**The baby became the princess' son,
and she named him Moses.**

Based on Exodus 2:10

God Speaks to Moses

Based on 3:1–5:21; 14:1–16:36

Moses was caring for his father-in-law's flock.

Based on Exodus 3:1

**Moses saw a bush that burned
with fire, but did not burn up.**

Based on Exodus 3:2

**When Moses looked at the bush,
God spoke to him.**

Based on Exodus 3:4

**God told Moses to take off his shoes because
he was standing on holy ground.**

Based on Exodus 3:5

God told Moses to lead the Israelites out of Egypt.

Based on Exodus 3:10

Moses and his brother Aaron went to Pharaoh and told him that God wanted the king to let the Israelites go.

Based on Exodus 5:1

The king said he would not let the people leave Egypt.

Based on Exodus 5:2

When the king heard that the people had fled, he got his chariot and his army and went after them.

Based on Exodus 14:5-8

When the Israelites saw the Egyptian army coming after them, they were afraid.

Based on Exodus 14:10

Moses told the Israelites to not be afraid because God would fight for them.

Based on Exodus 14:13, 14

God told Moses to lift up his rod and stretch out his hand over the sea.

Based on Exodus 14:16

When Moses obeyed God, the waters of the sea divided so the Israelites could walk through on dry land.

Based on Exodus 14:21, 22

**Because God protected them, Moses and
the Israelites sang praises to God.**

Based on Exodus 15:1-18

**After the Israelites crossed the Red Sea,
Moses led them into the wilderness.**

Based on Exodus 15:22

While in the wilderness, the Israelites started to complain because they had nothing to eat.

Based on Exodus 16:2, 3

God sent down bread like rain from Heaven.

Based on Exodus 16:4

The Ten Commandments

Based on Exodus 20:1-17; 24:12

God told Moses to go up the mountain where he would get tablets of stone with the laws God had written.

Based on Exodus 24:12

1. Do not worship any god except me.
2. Do not worship any object.
3. Do not misuse my name.
4. Remember the Sabbath Day belongs to me.
5. Respect your father and your mother.

6. Do not murder.
7. Be faithful in marriage.
8. Do not steal.
9. Do not tell lies.
10. Do not want what belongs to someone else.

Based on Exodus 20:1-17

The Story of Ruth

Based on Ruth 1:1–4:13

Naomi and her two daughters-in-law decided to leave Moab and go to Judah.

Based on Ruth 1:7

Ruth said she was going to stay with Naomi. Naomi's people would become her people and Naomi's God would be her God.

Based on Ruth 1:16

Naomi and Ruth traveled until they reached Bethlehem, and the whole city was happy to see them.

Based on Ruth 1:19

Naomi had a wealthy relative named Boaz. Ruth started picking up grain in a field owned by Boaz.

Based on Ruth 2:1, 3

Boaz went over and talked to Ruth.

Based on Ruth 2:8

Boaz invited Ruth to come eat with him.

Based on Ruth 2:14

Ruth ate all she wanted and still had extra food.

Based on Ruth 2:14

**Ruth took the extra food home
and gave it to Naomi.**

Based on Ruth 2:18

Ruth continued to work in the fields.

Based on Ruth 2:23

**Ruth and Boaz were married,
and God gave them a son.**

Based on Ruth 4:13

Hannah and Samuel

Based on 1 Samuel 1:1-28

Hannah prayed for a son.
She promised to give her son to God.

Based on 1 Samuel 1:11

God remembered Hannah's prayer and blessed her with a son. Hannah named her son Samuel.

Based on 1 Samuel 1:19, 20

When Samuel was still very young, Hannah took him to the house of God in Shiloh.

Based on 1 Samuel 1:24

GOD Appears to Samuel

Based on 1 Samuel 3:1-21

Samuel served God by helping Eli.

Based on 1 Samuel 3:1

**One night when Samuel was sleeping
God called out to him.**

Based on 1 Samuel 3:3, 4

**Samuel thought it was Eli who
had called out to him, so he ran to Eli.**

Based on 1 Samuel 3:5

Eli said he had not called Samuel and told Samuel to go back to bed.

Based on 1 Samuel 3:5

**God called out to Samuel two more times,
and Samuel kept going back to Eli.**

Based on 1 Samuel 3:7, 8

**After the third time, Eli realized
God had called for Samuel.**

Based on 1 Samuel 3:8

**Then God called him again, and Samuel said,
"Speak, for your servant hears you."**

Based on 1 Samuel 3:10

As Samuel grew, God was with him.

Based on 1 Samuel 3:19

David Becomes King

Based on 1 Samuel 16:1-23

God sent Samuel to visit Jesse because God had chosen one of Jesse's sons to become the next king.

Based on 1 Samuel 16:1

**Samuel did what the God told him
to do and went to Bethlehem.**

Based on 1 Samuel 16:4

Jesse had seven of his sons walk by Samuel.

Based on 1 Samuel 16:10

Samuel asked Jesse, "Are all of your children here? None of these is the one the God has chosen."

Based on 1 Samuel 16:10, 11

Jesse sent for his youngest son, David, who was taking care of the sheep.

Based on 1 Samuel 16:11, 12

**As his brothers watched, Samuel
took the horn of oil and anointed David king.**

Based on 1 Samuel 16:13

The Spirit of God came upon David.

Based on 1 Samuel 16:13

**The Spirit of God left King Saul,
and an evil spirit troubled him.**

Based on 1 Samuel 16:14

**Saul's servants decided to find a man who
could play the harp for Saul whenever
the evil spirit came upon him.**

Based on 1 Samuel 16:15, 16

**David came to King Saul and became
one of his servants.**

Based on 1 Samuel 16:21

Whenever the evil spirit came upon Saul, David would play his harp.

Based on 1 Samuel 16:23

David and Goliath

Based on 1 Samuel 17:1-54

Goliath, a Philistine, came out every morning and evening for forty days and challenged the Israelite army.

Based on 1 Samuel 17:16

One morning, David went to visit the soldiers as his father had told him to do.

Based on 1 Samuel 17:20

David saw how the Israelite soldiers fled from Goliath because they were afraid.

Based on 1 Samuel 17:24

David told King Saul that he would fight Goliath.

Based on 1 Samuel 17:32

**With his sling in his hand,
David went to meet Goliath.**

Based on 1 Samuel 17:40

**David put a stone in his sling
and swung the sling around.**

Based on 1 Samuel 17:49

Goliath fell facedown to the ground.

Based on 1 Samuel 17:49

The Story of Esther

Based on Esther 2–9

**King Xerxes of Persia loved Esther,
and he made her the queen.**

Based on Esther 2:17

In honor of Esther, the king made a great feast for his leaders and officials.

Based on Esther 2:18

Esther's uncle Mordecai had told her not to tell anyone that she was a Jew.

Based on Esther 2:19, 20

Two of the king's servants, Bigthan and Teresh, decided to kill the king.

Based on Esther 2:21

Mordecai learned about the plot, and he told Queen Esther to tell the king.

Based on Esther 2:22

**Later, King Xerxes promoted Haman to
the highest position in the kingdom.**

Based on Esther 3:1

Because Mordecai was a Jew, he would not bow to Haman. This made Haman angry.

Based on Esther 3:2-5

Haman convinced the king to order that every Jew in the kingdom be destroyed.

Based on Esther 3:6-10

When Mordecai heard this, he tore his clothes and cried with a loud cry.

Based on Esther 4:1

Esther told one of her servants to find out why Mordecai was acting like this.

Based on Esther 4:5

Mordecai told Esther's servant that Esther needed to go to the king. She needed to ask him to have mercy on the Jewish people.

Based on Esther 4:8

**Esther put on her royal robes
and went to see the king.**

Based on Esther 5:1

**When the king saw Queen Esther,
he was happy and held out the gold scepter.**

Based on Esther 5:2

Esther asked the king to come with Haman to a banquet she was preparing for them.

Based on Esther 5:4

At the banquet, the king told Esther he would give her anything she wanted.

Based on Esther 7:2

Esther asked the king to save her people, the Jews. She told him Haman was their enemy.

Based on Esther 7:3-6

**In anger, the king got up
and went to the palace garden.**

Based on Esther 7:7

The king made a law that the Jews could get together and defend themselves against others who tried to harm them.

Based on Esther 8:9-13

**The Jewish people were saved
and celebrated with a feast!**

Based on Esther 9:18-26

Psalms of Praise

**Because of you, God, I will be glad and rejoice.
I will sing praises to your name.**

Based on Psalm 9:2

The Lord is my shepherd; I shall not want.

Based on Psalm 23:1

God, I will not be afraid when I walk through the
darkest valley because I know you are with me.
Your rod and staff will comfort me.

Based on Psalm 23:4

Sing and play tambourines and pleasant-sounding stringed instruments to God.

Based on Psalm 81:2

Praise God with a trumpet.

God gives us springs in the valleys among the hills.

════════════ *Based on Psalm 104:10* ════════════

Because of you, God, the birds of the heavens build their nests and sing among the branches.

Based on Psalm 104:12

**God, your works are great;
the earth is full of your creations.**

Based on Psalm 104:24

Daniel and the Lions

Based on Daniel 6:1-24

**King Darius appointed Daniel ruler
over all the princes of the empire.**

Based on Daniel 6:1-3

The other princes tried to find fault with the way Daniel did his job.

Based on Daniel 6:4

The princes asked King Darius to make a law that no person could pray to God for thirty days. Whoever prayed during those thirty days would be put into the lions' den.

Based on Daniel 6:6, 7

**King Darius signed the law that said
no person could pray to God.**

Based on Daniel 6:9

When Daniel heard the law had been signed, he went home and prayed to God in front of an open window just as he always had done.

Based on Daniel 6:10

Daniel's enemies got together and watched Daniel pray. Then they told the king.

**When the king heard about Daniel praying,
he was upset and worked all day to
try to find a way to save Daniel.**

Based on Daniel 6:14

**King Darius commanded Daniel
be put into the lions' den.**

Based on Daniel 6:16

**After Daniel was put in the lions' den,
a stone was laid over the opening.**

Based on Daniel 6:17

Because Daniel was in the lions' den, the king spent the night without eating or sleeping.

Based on Daniel 6:18

**Early the next morning, the king got
up and ran to the lions' den.**

Based on Daniel 6:19

The king shouted, "Daniel, was your God able to save you from the lions?"

Based on Daniel 6:20

**Then Daniel said, "The lions have not hurt me.
My God sent an angel to shut the lions' mouths."**

Based on Daniel 6:22

The king commanded that Daniel be taken out of the lions' den.

Based on Daniel 6:23

The king commanded that the men who had accused Daniel be thrown into the lions' den.

Based on Daniel 6:24

Jonah and the Big Fish

God told Jonah to go to Nineveh and speak to the people because they were very wicked.

Based on Jonah 1:1, 2

Instead of doing what God said, Jonah got on a ship going to Tarshish—away from Nineveh.

Based on Jonah 1:3

**God sent a great wind, and
the ship was about to break apart.**

Based on Jonah 1:4

The sailors were afraid, and each man cried out to his god.

Based on Jonah 1:5

Jonah was fast asleep inside the ship.

Based on Jonah 1:5

The ship's captain went to Jonah and told him to wake up and call upon his God.

Based on Jonah 1:6

The sailors asked Jonah who he was, where he was from, and if he was the cause of the storm.

Based on Jonah 1:8

Jonah told the sailors to throw him into the sea to make it calm again.

Based on Jonah 1:12

**The sailors threw Jonah into the sea,
and the sea calmed down.**

Based on Jonah 1:15

God sent a big fish to swallow Jonah.

Based on Jonah 1:17

**Jonah was in the belly of the fish for
three days and three nights.**

Based on Jonah 1:17

**Jonah prayed and told
God he would obey him.**

Based on Jonah 2:1-9

God spoke to the big fish, and the big fish spat Jonah out onto dry land.

Based on Jonah 2:10

So Jonah obeyed God and went to Nineveh.

Based on Jonah 3:3

**Jonah told the people that God
would destroy Nineveh in forty days.**

Based on Jonah 3:4

**When God saw that the people of Nineveh had turned
from their evil ways, he had compassion
and did not destroy them.**

Based on Jonah 3:10

An Angel Speaks to Mary

Based on Luke 1:26-38

God sent an angel named Gabriel to a city in Galilee called Nazareth. God had a message for Mary.

Based on Luke 1:26, 27

The angel told Mary not to be afraid. Mary had found favor with God, and was going to have a baby.

Based on Luke 1:30

**Mary said, "I am the servant of the Lord!
Let whatever happens be according to your word."**

Based on Luke 1:38

The Birth of Jesus

Based on Luke 2:1-21; Matthew 2:1-12

**Mary and Joseph had to travel from Nazareth
to Bethlehem to be taxed.**

Based on Luke 2:3, 4

While they were there, Mary gave birth to her firstborn son.

Based on Luke 2:6, 7

Mary laid the baby in a manger, because there was no room for them to stay in the inn.

Based on Luke 2:7

The night Jesus was born, there were shepherds watching over their flocks in the field.

Based on Luke 2:8

An angel told the shepherds, "A Savior has been born today in the city of David. He is Christ the Lord."

Based on Luke 2:10, 11

The shepherds hurried off and found Mary, Joseph, and the baby lying in a manger.

Based on Luke 2:16

After Jesus was born in Bethlehem, some wise men came to Jerusalem to find him.

Based on Matthew 2:1-2

The wise men followed a star they had seen until it stopped over the place where Jesus was.

Based on Matthew 2:9

When the wise men came into the house, they saw Jesus with Mary. They fell down and worshiped him.

Based on Matthew 2:11

The wise men gave Jesus gifts of gold, frankincense, and myrrh.

Based on Matthew 2:11

Jesus in the Temple

Based on Luke 2:41-52

When Jesus was twelve years old, he went with his parents to Jerusalem to celebrate the Passover Feast.

Based on Luke 2:41, 42

**After the feast, Jesus' parents left to go home,
but Jesus stayed behind in Jerusalem. His parents
thought he was traveling with some other people.**

Based on Luke 2:43, 44

When Jesus' parents could not find him, they returned
to Jerusalem. They found Jesus in the temple, listening
to the teachers and asking questions.

Based on Luke 2:45, 46

**Everyone who heard Jesus was amazed
at his understanding and answers.**

Based on Luke 2:47

**Jesus went with home with parents
and always obeyed them.**

Based on Luke 2:51, 52

As Jesus grew, he became wise. He found favor with God and people.

Based on Luke 2:52

John the Baptist

**John's clothes were made of camel's hair.
He ate locusts and wild honey.**

Based on Mark 1:6

John told the people, "Someone mightier is coming after me."

Based on Mark 1:7

John said, "I have baptized you with water,
but he will baptize you with the Holy Spirit!"

Based on Mark 1:8

**Jesus came from Nazareth,
and John baptized him in the Jordan River.**

Based on Mark 1:9

When Jesus came out of the water, he saw the Spirit descending upon him like a dove.

Based on Mark 1:10

Jesus Chooses Four Fishermen

Based on Matthew 4:18-22

While Jesus was walking by the Sea of Galilee, he saw two brothers, Peter and Andrew.

Based on Matthew 4:18

Peter and Andrew were throwing their net into the water because they were fishermen.

Based on Matthew 4:18

Jesus said to Peter and Andrew, "Follow me, and I will make you fishers of men."

Based on Matthew 4:19

Jesus walked on and saw two more brothers, James and John, in a boat with their father.

Based on Matthew 4:21

Jesus called to James and John to come with him too. They left their nets and followed him.

Based on Matthew 4:21, 22

Jesus Heals a Man Who Can't Walk

Based on Mark 2:1-12

Jesus went to Capernaum, and a few days later people heard that he was in a house.

Based on Mark 2:1

Soon there were so many people gathered at the house that there was no more room.

Based on Mark 2:2

While Jesus was preaching about God, four men came to the house, carrying a man on a mat. The man could not walk.

Based on Mark 2:2, 3

When the four men couldn't get through the crowd, they made a hole in the roof above Jesus and let down the mat in front of everyone.

Based on Mark 2:4

When Jesus saw the men's faith, he told the man on the mat to stand, pick up the mat, and go home. And the man did!

Based on Mark 2:5, 11, 12

Jesus Chooses His Twelve Apostles

Based on Mark 3:13-19

Jesus went up on a mountain, and asked
some of his followers to go with him.

Based on Mark 3:13

**Jesus chose twelve of the followers to be with him.
He would send them out to preach.**

Based on Mark 3:14

The twelve were Peter, James, John, Andrew, Philip, Bartholomew,

Based on Mark 3:16-19

Matthew, Thomas, James, Thaddaeus, Simon, and Judas.

Based on Mark 3:16-19

A Widow's Son

Based on Luke 7:11-17

Jesus and his disciples went to a city called Nain, and many people came with them.

Based on Luke 7:11

When Jesus came to the gate of the city, there was a dead man being carried out. He was the only son of a widow.

Based on Luke 7:12

Jesus went over and touched the coffin.

Jesus said, "Young man, I tell you, get up."
The dead son sat up and began talking.

Based on Luke 7:14, 15

**Jesus gave the son who had been
dead back to his mother.**

Based on Luke 7:15

A Storm

Based on Matthew 8:23-27

One day Jesus and his disciples got in a boat to cross the lake. Suddenly, a terrible storm came upon the lake.

Based on Matthew 8:23, 24

Jesus fell asleep in the boat. The disciples woke Jesus.

Based on Matthew 8:24, 25

The disciples said, "Jesus, save us.
We're going to drown!"

Based on Matthew 8:25

Getting to his feet, Jesus told the wind, "Silence!" and the waves, "Quiet down!" And the wind and waves obeyed him.

Based on Matthew 8:26

Jesus Feeds Five Thousand

Based on John 6:1-13

Jesus went across the Sea of Galilee.

Based on John 6:1

Jesus saw a crowd following him. He asked Philip, "Where can we buy bread to feed these people?"

Based on John 6:5

Philip said, "Two hundred silver pieces wouldn't be enough to buy bread for all of these people."

Based on John 6:7

Andrew said, "Here's a little boy who has five barley loaves and two small fish."

Based on John 6:8, 9

Jesus said, "Make the people sit down."
There were about 5,000 men.

Based on John 6:10

Jesus took the bread and gave thanks to God.

Based on John 6:11

Jesus gave the bread to the disciples, and the disciples gave bread to those who were seated. Jesus did the same with the fish.

Based on John 6:11

All of the people ate until they were full.

Jesus told the disciples to gather the leftovers so nothing would be wasted. There were twelve baskets of food left over.

Based on John 6:12, 13

The Woman of Great Faith

Based on Luke 7:36-50

A Pharisee wanted Jesus to eat with him, so Jesus went to the Pharisee's house.

Based on Luke 7:36

**A woman who had led a sinful life
came and stood at Jesus' feet.**

Based on Luke 7:37, 38

The woman began to wash Jesus' feet with her tears and wipe them with her hair.

Based on Luke 7:38

**The woman kissed Jesus' feet and
anointed them with ointment.**

Based on Luke 7:38

The Pharisee said to himself, "If Jesus were a prophet, he would know that this woman is a sinner."

Based on Luke 7:39

**Jesus told the woman, "Your faith
has saved you; go in peace."**

Based on Luke 7:50

Jesus Walks on the Water

Based on Matthew 14:22-33

**Jesus told his disciples to get in a
ship without him and go to the other side.**

Based on Matthew 14:22

After Jesus had sent the crowd away, he went up on a mountain to pray. Evening came and Jesus was alone.

Based on Matthew 14:22, 23

While the disciples were in the ship, a strong wind came up and tossed the ship around in the waves.

Based on Matthew 14:24

Jesus went to his disciples by walking on the water.

Based on Matthew 14:25

When the disciples saw Jesus walking on the water, they thought he was a ghost. But Jesus told them not to be afraid.

Based on Matthew 14:26, 27

Peter said, "Lord, if it is you,
tell me to come to you on the water."

Based on Matthew 14:28

"Come!" Jesus said to Peter.

Based on Matthew 14:29

**Peter got out of the ship and walked to Jesus.
But when Peter saw the strong wind,
he was afraid and began to sink.**

Based on Matthew 14:29, 30

Immediately Jesus reached out his hand to Peter. Jesus said, "Oh you of little faith."

Based on Matthew 14:31

**Those on the ship worshiped Jesus, saying,
"You are the Son of God."**

Based on Matthew 14:33

The Good Samaritan

Based on Luke 10:25-37

Jesus told a story about a man who went down from Jerusalem to Jericho. Some thieves beat him up and then left him.

Based on Luke 10:30

**A priest came that way, and when he
saw the man, he passed by on the other side.**

Based on Luke 10:31

A Levite came and looked at the man, and passed by on the other side.

Based on Luke 10:32

**A Samaritan came by, and when
he saw the man he felt sorry for him.**

Based on Luke 10:33

**The Samaritan poured oil on the man's
wounds and then he bandaged them.**

Based on Luke 10:34

The Samaritan put the man on his own donkey and brought him to an inn, where he took care of him.

Based on Luke 10:34

Jesus asked, "Which of these three do you think was a neighbor to the man who fell among thieves? Go and do the same."

Based on Luke 10:36, 37

Two Sons

Based on Luke 15:11-32

Jesus told a story. A man had two sons. The younger son wanted the share of his father's money that would one day belong to him.

Based on Luke 15:11, 12

A few days later the younger son packed up everything he owned and took a journey far away.

Based on Luke 15:13

When the son had spent all he had, a mighty famine came upon the land.

Based on Luke 15:14

The younger son decided to go back to his father and work as a servant.

Based on Luke 15:18, 19

The father saw his son coming. When the son was still a long way off, the father ran to him and hugged and kissed him.

Based on Luke 15:20

The son said, "I have sinned against God and you.
I am not worthy to be called your son."

Based on Luke 15:21

The father told the servants, "Bring the best robe, and put it on my son. Put a ring on his hand, and shoes on his feet."

Based on Luke 15:22

And there was a big celebration.

The older son asked a servant what was going on, and the servant told him that his brother had returned home.

Based on Luke 15:26, 27

**The older brother got angry and
would not go to the celebration.**

Based on Luke 15:28

The older son said to his father, "For many years I have served you and have always obeyed you."

Based on Luke 15:29

The father said, "All that I have is yours.
Your brother was dead and is alive again."

Based on Luke 15:31, 32

Jesus Blesses Little Children

Based on Mark 10:13-16

Some people brought young children to Jesus so he could touch them.

Based on Mark 10:13

**The disciples told the people
not to bother Jesus.**

Based on Mark 10:13

Jesus said, "Let the children come to me."

Based on Mark 10:14

Jesus said, "These children are the kingdom of God."

Based on Mark 10:14

**Jesus took the children in
his arms and blessed them.**

Based on Mark 10:16

Jesus Heals Two Men Who Are Blind

Based on Matthew 20:29-34

**When Jesus and his disciples left Jericho,
a large crowd followed them.**

Based on Matthew 20:29

Two men who were blind were sitting by the side of the road. They cried out to Jesus, "Lord, have mercy on us."

Based on Matthew 20:30

**The crowd told the men who were blind
to be quiet, but they cried louder.**

Based on Matthew 20:31

Jesus stopped and called to the men who were blind, asking what they wanted him to do.

Based on Matthew 20:32

The two men said to Jesus, "Lord, we want to see."

Based on Matthew 20:33

Jesus felt sorry for the two men and touched their eyes. Immediately, they could see and they followed Jesus.

Based on Matthew 20:34

Jesus Enters Jerusalem

Based on Matthew 21:1-11

When Jesus and his disciples came close to Jerusalem, he sent two disciples ahead to bring him a donkey.

Based on Matthew 21:1, 2

The disciples went and did what Jesus said to do.

Based on Matthew 21:6

Jesus got on the donkey.

Based on Matthew 21:7

**Many people spread their garments
on the road, while others cut down branches
and spread them in the way.**

Based on Matthew 21:8

All the people were shouting praises to Jesus.

Based on Matthew 21:9

Jesus in the Temple

Based on Matthew 21:12-17

Jesus went to the temple of God and chased out everyone who was selling and buying.

Based on Matthew 21:12

He turned over the tables of the money changers.

Based on Matthew 21:12

Jesus told the people that the temple is a house of prayer.

Based on Matthew 21:13

People who could not see or walk came to Jesus in the temple, and he healed them.

Based on Matthew 21:14

Jesus Eats with His Disciples

Based on Luke 22:7-23

Jesus told Peter and John to go and prepare the Passover meal.

Based on Luke 22:8

**Peter and John found everything
just as Jesus had told them.**

Based on Luke 22:13

Jesus took a cup and gave thanks to God.

Based on Luke 22:17

Jesus took some bread and gave thanks for it.

Based on Luke 22:19

Life Among the Lord's Followers

Based on Acts 2:43-47

Everyone was amazed at the wonders and signs done by the apostles.

Based on Acts 2:43

All those who believed in Jesus were together, and they shared all they had.

Based on Acts 2:44

The believers sold their possessions and goods and gave the money to whoever needed it.

Based on Acts 2:45

The believers met in homes and ate together, happily sharing their food.

Based on Acts 2:46

With God's Power, Peter and John Heal a Man

Based on Acts 3:1-10

Peter and John went to the temple to pray.

Based on Acts 3:1

A man who had never been able to walk had been carried and laid at the gate of the temple.

Based on Acts 3:2

The man asked Peter and John for money.

Peter said, "In the name of Jesus Christ
of Nazareth, stand up and walk."

Based on Acts 3:6

**The man who had not been able to walk
jumped up and began to walk.**

Based on Acts 3:8

The healed man went with Peter and John into the temple, walking and leaping and praising God.

Based on Acts 3:8

Saul Preaches in Damascus

Based on Acts 9:19-25

Saul stayed several days with Jesus' disciples in Damascus.

Based on Acts 9:19

Saul preached with such power that he confused the Jewish people living in Damascus.

Based on Acts 9:22

**Some Jews made plans to kill Saul,
but Saul found out about it.**

Based on Acts 9:23, 24

**The Jews who wanted to kill Saul
watched the gates of the city day and night.**

Based on Acts 9:24

**One night, some disciples helped Saul
escape over the city wall in a basket.**

Based on Acts 9:25

Paul in Athens

Based on Acts 17:16-34

When Paul was in Athens, he became very upset because the city was full of idols.

Based on Acts 17:16

**Day after day Paul spoke about Jesus
in the market with everyone he met.**

Based on Acts 17:17

**The people of Athens brought Paul
before a group of powerful men.**

Based on Acts 17:19

The powerful men asked Paul to tell them about the new ideas he was teaching.

Based on Acts 17:19

**Paul said that God is not
an idol made out of gold or silver.**

Based on Acts 17:29

Some of the people believed what Paul was saying and put their faith in God.

Based on Acts 17:34

The Shipwreck

Based on Acts 27:13-44

Shortly after some sailors set sail, a strong wind came up. There were 276 people on the ship, including Paul.

Based on Acts 27:14, 37

**The sailors could not steer the ship,
so they let the wind carry them.**

Based on Acts 27:15

**For many days, the people on the ship
could not see the sun or the stars.**

Based on Acts 27:20

**One morning, the sailors saw land
they did not recognize.**

Based on Acts 27:39

The sailors wanted to sail toward the land.

Based on Acts 27:39

The wind carried the ship toward the shore.

Based on Acts 27:40

**The front of the ship stuck firmly in the sand,
and the rear was smashed by the waves.**

Based on Acts 27:41

**Everyone who could swim was
ordered to jump into the water.**

Based on Acts 27:42, 43

**Those who could not swim were
told to hold onto planks of wood.**

Based on Acts 27:44

Everyone made it safely to land.

Based on Acts 27:44

A Prophecy from John

Based on Revelation 1; 21:10, 11

Jesus sent his angel to his servant John with a message about things that would happen in the future.

Based on Revelation 1:1

God will bless everyone who reads and hears the words of John's prophecy.

Based on Revelation 1:3

John heard a voice speaking to him. When he turned to see who was speaking, he saw seven golden candlesticks.

Based on Revelation 1:10-12

**There with the candlesticks was someone
like the Son of Man. The voice told
John to write down what he saw.**

Based on Revelation 1:13, 19

**The angel showed John the holy
city coming from Heaven.**

Based on Revelation 21:10